Happy Inside Out

Andrea Ince

Published by New Generation Publishing in 2022

First Edition

ISBN

| | Paperback | 978-1-80369-164-0 |
| | Hardback | 978-1-80369-165-7 |

www.newgeneration-publishing.com

New Generation Publishing

Anyone can appear happy on the outside but being Happy Inside Out, can literally change your life!

Happy Inside Out is about that warm feeling inside, deep down in your belly, like an inner glow.

Acknowledgements

To my husband Stuart, my children Chloe and Davis and my closest friends and family – thank you for believing in me that I could do this.

Thank you to Michael Heppell for his inspiration and enthusiasm in setting up that first Write That Book Masterclass during 2020 and all that is Team 17. I have learnt a lot from Michael about myself and met some amazing people through being a member of Team 17, who have encouraged me to keep going and get my book published (you know who you are).

Contents

Introduction

Happy Inside Out is about that warm feeling inside, deep down in your belly like an inner glow. Often, we are so busy making sure everyone else is happy and even though we may appear happy on the outside, we forget to think about our inner self, and what we truly need to be happy. Happiness is also different things to different people and is about being true to yourself.

Happy Inside Out looks at all areas of your life: you, family, friends, work, thoughts, and dreams. It helps you to work 'you' out, as we are all unique. You would not bake a cake with just a single ingredient – Happy Inside Out is about looking at all areas of your mind and life; working on them, so they work together to create a feeling of happiness both inside and out.

The book is also about how to recognise unhappiness - working out why you feel unhappy and doing something about that feeling of unhappiness rather than accepting it. Allowing you to turn that unhappy feeling into a happy one.

When you start to think about all of this, you can start to understand and train yourself to do and say things that make you HAPPY INSIDE OUT. It works, trust me!

Some days I feel happy,
Some days I feel sad,
And some days I'm not sure how I feel,
And that can make me feel quite mad.

But then I make sure I speak to 'me'
All you can do is your best,
If your best isn't good enough for something,
Let it be and get on with the rest!

By Andrea Ince

I finished writing my book on World Book Day 2021!!!!!!
x

Part 1

What makes you happy?

What makes you happy? That is a very good place to start. Think about the words you use; how do they make you feel? Are you happier around certain people? Why is that do you think?

What does being happy mean to you? Now this is quite different to the first question and sometimes where we go wrong. If anyone ever tells you that being happy is a single thing, DO NOT believe them!

Sit down and think about it for 5 minutes – are you really happy, or are you just telling yourself you are happy? There is an enormous difference. You can never really be Happy Inside Out unless you are genuinely happy.

Being happy can be an object, a scene, a photo, an action, a person, a film, a memory, all of these and so much more…. Being happy is all about that lovely warm tingly feeling inside that makes you literally smile from the inside out.

When you are happy, your aura around you is happy too, which encourages more happiness to come your way. Have you ever noticed that when you are feeling a little low, the mood around you, and the feeling in the air feels low and heavy too? When you are feeling unhappy, conversations with others can also feel subdued. However, when you feel happy, there is more happiness around you – everywhere!

Ten things to help you be happy:

1. Call someone that you have been meaning to call for a long while.

2. Smile at people when you see them on your travels. You do not know what that person is feeling from the outside, and a friendly smile will make them feel better and I guarantee it will make you feel better too.

3. Have a nice warm bath, with some candles and relax.

4. Say hello to people that you pass in the street or at the shops. We always used to do this but not so much these days. I have done it a few times and sometimes the recipient has looked at me as if I were mad, which makes me chuckle.

5. Next time you see someone that is special to you, give them a big hug and tell them how special they are. This is the thing I have missed during the COVID-19 pandemic!

6. Invest in a little quotation book and every morning just see where the book opens.

7. Plan to do at least one thing a day for 'you' – no one else. It can be for as little time as 5 minutes, but I guarantee that however you were feeling, it will calm you down and change your mood for the better.

8. Arrange to meet up with friends and have a good old natter – good old natters usually encourage memories and often the giggles, as you reminisce happy events or situations.

9. Stop what you are doing and appreciate what is around you – the scenery, the objects, the sky, the people. Gratitude is a fabulous thing, and everyone has something they are grateful for, even if that grateful thing is for just being alive.

10. Think about where your Happy Place is and when things get a bit tense or rocky, take yourself there, even if it is only in your mind – This is one of my favourite ones.

Think about YOU

Sometimes it is so easy to put everyone else before yourself, but it is so important to have that 'ME' time when you can do something just for you. Often doing that will make you feel guilty that you haven't done this or that, but those other jobs will still be there after you have had your 'ME' time. Having time for you helps you to realign and I will guarantee that you will feel happier inside and calmer when you have made the effort and taken some time out for you.

What you do in your 'ME' time is entirely up to you, and everybody will have something different that makes them STOP - a bit like the way happiness is different for everyone too. Have that bath, read that book, go for a run, walk the dog, do 10 mins of browsing online shopping, sort out your wardrobe, call or message your best friend. When you have done it, you will feel happy!

We have all done this I guarantee, and anyone that says they haven't is telling fibs. When someone asks you if you are OK, have you ever said "Yes, I'm fine" or "OK" even if you feel rubbish and down inside? Sometimes you may have even said you are happy because you know this is what the other person wants to hear.

This is dangerous and all it does is builds up the tension inside your body and pushes that happiness further away. Sometimes you can do this so much, what happens is you convince yourself that you are happy, even if you are not. Whether that be relationships, work, family, it is so important to be honest with yourself, if you cannot be honest with yourself, who can you be honest with?

There is only one of you and you are unique. What makes you happy is different from what makes your partner happy or your friend happy and that is the way it should be. Some people love to journal, some love quotations, some love to talk, some people just keep their happiness to themselves. Whatever you do that is fine – you are unique.

Happiness is something that is free, and once you are Happy Inside Out, you can stretch your wings and do whatever it is that you want or need to.

"Be yourself; everyone else is already taken."

Unknown

As you look at this more, you will realise the very thing or things that make you happy. This may change too – life changes and so do you.

Have you ever looked in the mirror and thought?

"If only I was more like that…!" or "If only I was more like that person?"

Well, there is good news – you can be! With the amount of social media pressure in the present day, we may easily find ourselves under pressure to post that 'ideal' life. However, we should remember, some people post because that makes them happy, some people post to gloss over the cracks that might be happening in their life, and some people live their lives in the public domain because it makes them look better and that may even make them feel better about themselves.

But……. does it?

Are the people that live their lives on social media Happy Inside Out? Now that is the question you should be asking.

Nine times out of ten, the answer will be no they are not Happy Inside Out.

Someone once told me that you should never accept a connection on LinkedIn unless you were willing to invite that person into your home for a cup of tea. It is crazy how there are so many companies that will sell you connections on social media channels. Some people like to welcome these people into their lives but just be careful.

It is important to spend some time on yourself each and every day. Whether that be for 5 minutes sat quietly, just to think and reassess, or a whole hour of doing that chore or job that you have been meaning to do for months if not years. Seven days of just 5 minutes per day is 35 mins per week and I guarantee you will feel happier at the end of the week.

Be grateful – say it aloud and feel the difference. Different philosophers tell you to do your gratitude this way and that but do it your way. Be unique and you will feel the happiness inside rather than turning being happy into a chore.

You cannot be genuinely happy if you are not doing what you truly want to do. Be Yourself!

Learn to let go of things that no longer serve you. This will lead the way and give you space to fill your time with things that do serve you and make you feel happy. Sometimes it is extremely hard to let go, but you need to trust your intuition and ride the new feeling of doing something new.

Think back to when you are a baby – all you know is laying but then you learn to sit up, and then you learn to crawl which leads to walking with something and then one day, you are walking on your own. You can use that analogy for what makes you happy. There is no need to hold onto things for dear life just because. Go on give it a go.

Do not be worried about what other people think. Be you, there is no-one quite like you!

"Be yourself; everyone else is already taken."

Unknown

I'll be happy when…….

"Most people are about as happy as they make up their mind to be."

Abraham Lincoln

Many people live their lives treating happiness like a destination. They say "I will be happy when….." treating happiness like arriving at a pre-decided destination after a long drive. But life isn't like that.

I am not saying that you cannot plan or have a dream for the future, but make sure you live your life and make the right decisions for the 'now' and not for the 'what if.'

There are more and more real-life stories about people that have enjoyed long and successful careers but then they suddenly retire and unfortunately something happens. They have all those dreams and plans of being Happy Inside Out when they retire because they can now do some of the things that they honestly believe will make them happier and BAM…….., their lives are cut short, and they leave this planet not having done the things that they believe will make them Happy Inside Out.

I have found this poem by a lady called Linda Ellis and it is so powerful:

The Dash

I read of a man who stood to speak at the funeral of a friend,
He referred to the dates on the tombstone, from the beginning to the end.
He noted that first came the date of birth and spoke of the following date with tears,

11

But he said what mattered most of all was the dash between those years.
For that dash represents all the time that they spend alive on earth,
And now only those that loved them know what that little line is worth.
For it matters not how much we own, the cars, the house, the cash,
What matters is how we live and love and how we spend our dash.

So think about this long and hard, are there things you'd like to change?
For you never know how much time is left that can still be rearranged.
If we could just slow down enough to consider what's true and real
And always try to understand the way other people feel.

And be less quick to anger and show appreciation more
And love the people in our lives like we've never loved before.
If we treat each other with respect and more often wear a smile,
Remembering that this special dash may only last a while.

So when your eulogy is being read with your life's actions to rehash,
Would you be proud of the things they say about how you spent your dash?

Linda Ellis

When we are teenagers, we might say to ourselves, I will be happier when I finish school/college. We then start our employment careers and things are not how we thought they would be, and we start to think I will be happier when I get a new job, or I get my own house. Life carries on and you might be saying I will be happier when I settle down and find the love of my life. Then you might say, I will feel happier inside out when we have a family of our own which leads to, I can be happier and free to do the things I really want to do when the children leave home. You are then looking forward to retiring and being able to do all the things you have always wanted to do, that you believe will make you genuinely happy. **STOP**...........

Don't be one of those people. What is stopping us being Happy Inside Out when we are those school children, single people at the start of their career, young lovers, a family with young children, Mum's and Dad's having the extra time to themselves when their children leave home? Do you know what the answer to that question is? **YOU**.

You are the one that can make little changes right from when you are that worried teenager trying their best with their exams. These minor changes do not have to be huge. It may be as simple as giving yourself 5 minutes a day to think about what makes you happy at the present time and what makes you sad. Can you look at those sad thoughts and turn them into happy ones? Be completely honest with yourself and those around you. Talk to people whether that be family or friends.

Write things down that you want to achieve. At the beginning of each year, I write down a list of things that I would like to have done in the next year. Now that list does not have to be huge projects or way-out things but can be quite simple.

When I look at this list at the end of the year, yes, I feel pleased with myself if I have managed to cross off some of the items on the list, but I have learnt not to beat myself up inside if I have not managed to do some of them too.

Instead, I feel good that I have managed to do some and think "Well perhaps I will try that this year." That is so much better than thinking, "well I didn't do much of that did I?" I celebrate the fact I did some of the things, rather than feel bad and despondent that I did not complete all of my list. There is a lesson there for us all, I think you will agree.

You don't have to wait until the end of the year, month, or week, just make a list today and I guarantee you are then turning things around and you will start to feel more content and happier inside out!

"Most people are about as happy as they make up their mind to be."

Abraham Lincoln

What is in your filing cabinet in your head?

As we have said already, being Happy Inside Out means different things to different people.

One thing that can help you be Happy Inside Out is the memories that are stored away deep in your mind and subconscious. They are stored in your mind like a filing cabinet, and it is a great skill to be able to open that filing cabinet every once in a while and remind yourself of that feeling you had deep inside your body when that memory happened. Most of us have a 'Happy Place' in our memory filing cabinet. That memory of being in a certain place and how happy you felt or how happy the people around you were.

A great memory for me that is always guaranteed to put a smile on my face and make me feel happy inside and out, is a trip to Iceland with friends. We booked a coach trip to try and see the Northern Lights and a little 18-seater coach arrived outside the hotel. There were six of us and we may have had a few drinks before we left, as if anyone who has ever been to Iceland and booked one of these tours will know, they collect you late at night – it has to be dark after all!

We boarded the coach and straight away we knew we would have a good trip as the driver was a local man with a big personality – he reminded me of a Red Coat or the Children's Entertainers that I once worked with. He started the excursion by asking us all to stand up individually and tell the other coach passengers our name and where we were from. In our group, one of our friends introduced himself as 'Del Boy' from Essex (you know who you are!) and it was very funny listening to us all introduce ourselves to each other. A great ice breaker as we had Americans, Chinese, Germans, and a few French people on the coach.

We arrived at the viewing point in the middle of nowhere and we all had to get out. You stand there looking up at the dark sky and hope that you will see the Northern Lights. We waited and waited and waited for hours, and our host/driver advised us it may happen soon. It was freezing cold and many of our party got back on the bus and gave up.

Well, I consider myself to be a positive person and I had just completed a positive mindset course – I believed that the negativity of giving up and sitting back on the bus in the dark was not going to help us see the Northern Lights, so I got on the bus and asked everyone to get off and be positive about seeing the lights – in a nice way I promise. They must have thought I was a mad English lady but politely did as I asked. The coach driver loved this and when we were all once again outside staring at the dark sky, he suddenly announced that we should all stand in a circle and do the Okey Cokey! Well, if the group had thought I was mad asking them to get off the bus, now they were being asked to do the Okey Cokey by the driver – what a night. It was fantastic and something that I know I will never forget, and I am guessing the other passengers will never forget it either. There were no pictures, no videos – it was pitch black after all, but a fantastic memory which makes me smile just writing about it. In case you are wondering, we unfortunately did not see the Northern Lights!

Why am I telling you this? Well, that is a memory that I keep in my filing cabinet in my head as it always makes me feel Happy Inside Out. If I am feeling a little sad or stressed or just mewh, this is one of my 'go to' memories that I pull out and instantly fills me with an inner glow. I have lots of memories like these and I am sure you as the reader of this book has some too.

Have 5 minutes to yourself and think of the memories you can store in your Happy Inside Out folder in the filing cabinet of your brain and I guarantee you will get that warm feeling inside.

Let us talk some more about your filing cabinet in your mind. There is one thing that has happened to everyone and that is growing up! Now growing up can bring back happy memories and sad memories for some but concentrate on the happy ones. You cannot beat a chat with someone where you recall a childhood memory. If you are having 'one of those days' or are just feeling a little sad, stop what you are doing and open that filing cabinet at a childhood memory – always guaranteed to turn most unhappiness away and help to bring back those happy thoughts.

Another filing drawer could be a musical one. Music can make even the most boring job more bearable and boosts your energy and how happy you feel inside. Make a playlist of your 'Happy Inside Out' songs – guaranteed to lift your spirits, make you feel happier inside and make you sing aloud! Then, next time you are about to do a chore that you really hate or seems like it will take forever, stick on your happy playlist and it is guaranteed to not only help you get the chore done, but it will make the time it takes go quicker and lift your happiness inside.

11 Happy Songs

1. Happy by Pharrell Williams

2. Can't Stop the Feeling by Justin Timberlake

3. Shiny Happy People by R.E.M.

4. Walking on Sunshine by Katrina and the Waves

5. I Gotta Feeling by Black Eyed Peas

6. Don't Worry, Be Happy by Bobby McFerrin

7. Love My Life by Robbie Williams

8. Better When I'm Dancin' by Meghan Trainor

9. Dancing Queen by Abba

10. Shut Up and Dance by Walk the Moon

11. Respect by Erasure

Lists

Over the years I have tried using lists and not using lists and am a firm believer that you can be more in control of your whole life and happiness if you use lists. Now some may read that sentence and think it strange but just think about it for a few minutes.

Sometimes we use lists without even thinking about it for things like shopping or packing for a holiday (as this book is being written in the third National Lockdown of the COVID-19 pandemic of 2020/21, I really am missing writing a holiday packing list!). These lists help us to be organised and there is something quite rewarding when you have crossed that last item off the holiday packing list. That is the sort of moment when you get that smile inside and out, which is exactly the feeling this book is all about.

Some Personal Development Coaches will tell you that you should write lists every day of what you want to achieve that day, and some take this one step further and say that you should write a list the night before of the three things you would like to do the following day. I cannot acknowledge the person that came up with that idea, but I have heard it three times from three different coaches in the last month!

Personally, I think lists are important to focus and get stuff done, but you do have to be careful that you do not spend too much time writing lists and then not having the time to do the things on them. It is all about what works for you, what makes a difference and sometimes adapting the list making for yourself. Don't forget as I keep saying, we are all unique and have our own way of making lists work for us. If your lists make you happy and content – that is the important thing.

It is nice to make a list of things that make you smile, or a playlist of happy songs that you can quickly find if you are having a dip of energy or perhaps you are feeling sad. In this way lists become a quick pick up and are definitely a tool for being Happy Inside Out.

Lists can also work a little like your filing cabinet of memories stored in your head, as you could stop and make a list of happy memories which you could keep in a safe place and come back to, or perhaps share later with friends and family.

There are some that say, "Oh I keep lists in my head" That may work for them, but I think written lists work much better and give you much more satisfaction and happiness. I am not saying lists must be pen and paper, although they are my favourite, but using Notes on your phone is a fantastic way of making a list and having it to hand when you need it.

I make my Christmas Lists on my phone every year for what I am buying friends and family – it is so useful to have and works as a reminder as to what you bought the previous year for when I am having a 'Dory' moment!

I love lists and if you are serious about being Happy Inside Out, I would recommend you make more.

Writing

I love writing – in fact, I love words, which is good as it forms a big part of my day job. You might be interested to know that my day job is a Freelance Marketing and PR Consultant. Writing is incredibly good for the soul and lots of people find it very soothing. Writing can come in all forms and does not mean you have to write a book. Writing a book had never even been a thought in my head until I joined a Facebook Pop Up Group run by the brilliant Michael Heppell and the rest, as they say, is history…..

On our journey of finding happiness both inside and out, writing can play a big part. Lots of happy people swear by the fact that journaling every day helps them to be content and happy. Journaling is not just keeping a diary about what you have done, but it is also about writing down what you would have liked to do, your thoughts on the day, what you may have done differently and the big one for me is what you are grateful for.

Now some people just write a gratitude list every day about what they are grateful for, some just write what they have done, and some do something completely different. I believe that the most important thing to do is what feels right with you. If you try and journal all the above and it does not make you have that Happy Inside Out feeling, then perhaps what you are doing in your writing needs adjusting.

I do believe that writing things down helps you sit and think about things. We have already spoken about the usefulness of lists and writing down goals has been taught by Personal Development Coaches for years. If you speak to many successful people, they will all say that they write down their goals and aspirations. You do not need to do this every day, choose what suits you and see what happens.

There is no right or wrong, and we all need to believe in ourselves more to do what helps us. It once again goes back to originality and the fact that we are all different and at various stages of our journey/life. Do what is right for you and do not beat yourself up if you skip a day or more. Writing and journaling should not be a chore, it should naturally become part of your personal routine.

It is also worth remembering that throughout life, our circumstances change and that includes your needs and wants. I have learnt in the past couple of years that just because you have done something a certain way for yourself for what seems like forever, it does not mean that it cannot change. In fact, it is a good thing if it does change or evolve, as we all evolve through our lives, as we experience different things. What was important to you 5 or 10 years ago or even 1 year ago, may not be important to you now.

Friends and Family

Some of you may already know that I love my dog Bobby – being someone that had never had a dog, I cannot believe how he really is one of my best friends and follows me everywhere. I often talk to him when I am working or writing, and it was only right that I mention him in my book.

As humans, we have talked about being really happy and how you can sometimes mask how you are actually feeling inside. We are told that dogs are happy when they are wagging their tails but how do we know they are happy? Bobby thinks he is a cat and sometimes purrs like a cat which is a cat's way of being happy. Let's face it, we all think we know when our pets are happy but do we really know!? Pets are so clever; they really do know when you are happy or not and they cannot see inside your body or brain. If I am ever feeling a little blue, Bobby will be even more attentive than usual. Wouldn't it be great if we could do it with humans too?

It is so important to check in on family and friends to see how they are. Remember that how we feel often rubs off on the people around us, so if we are happy, then the people around us are happier or we can influence how happy they are. This can also work the other way – if you are not feeling happy, talking to someone who is happy may help you!

Do not be afraid to ask if someone is OK and don't be afraid to say how you really feel, not what you think that person wants to hear. Talking to friends and family is important!

It is also worth remembering that they say, people and friends come into your life for a reason, season, or a lifetime. There is a lovely poem about this:

People come into your life for a reason, a season, or a lifetime.

When you figure out which one it is,
you will know what to do for each person.

When someone is in your life for a REASON,
it is usually to meet a need you have expressed.
They have come to assist you through a difficulty;
to provide you with guidance and support;
to aid you physically, emotionally, or spiritually.
They may seem like a godsend, and they are.
They are there for the reason you need them to be.

Then, without any wrongdoing on your part or at an inconvenient time,
this person will say or do something to bring the relationship to an end.
Sometimes they die. Sometimes they walk away.
Sometimes they act up and force you to take a stand.
What we must realise is that our need has been met, our desire fulfilled; their work is done.
The prayer you sent up has been answered and now it is time to move on.

Some people come into your life for a SEASON,
because your turn has come to share, grow, or learn.
They bring you an experience of peace or make you laugh.
They may teach you something you have never done.
They usually give you an unbelievable amount of joy.
Believe it. It is real. But only for a season.

LIFETIME relationships teach you lifetime lessons;
things you must build upon in order to have a solid emotional foundation.
Your job is to accept the lesson, love the person,
and put what you have learned to use in all other

relationships and areas of your life.
It is said that love is blind but friendship is clairvoyant.

Unknown

Being Honest and Sometimes Unhappy

I thought it was only right to include a part of my book about being honest. Now when I say being honest, I do not mean saying actual words but more what you think.

Yes, this book is about being Happy Inside Out, but I would be the first to agree that it is very hard to be happy all the time. This is something that has cropped up in my social media page on Happy Inside Out. The secret is to be able to acknowledge truthfully that you are not feeling happy, whether that be on the inside or the outside and recognising what triggered that unhappiness.

It is also about being honest with the people that are around you, whether that be family, friends, or work colleagues. If those people around you do not realise that you are unhappy, then they cannot comfort you and help you to turn it around and be happy. Sometimes we think that we are showing people how we feel, but they are not always truly aware of your feelings.

If it is family, be honest, don't pretend. Sometimes a hug is all you need to scare the unhappiness back to where it came from. With friends, don't say you are OK if you are not – very good friends, your besties, are usually very aware of the 'true you' and how you are feeling, but I bet if we are all very honest, we have all said that we are OK and happy to our best friends at least once or twice, when actually what we are really feeling is less than happy.

Some people cover up that they are not happy, and others therefore perceive that person as being happy. Well nine times out of ten, that happy person has the same worries as you, whether that be feeling old, feeling like you don't have any nice clothes to wear, feeling tired and a bit low sometimes, the list could go on. We are all unique but lots of us have the same worries. Sometimes admitting that you have these worries and hearing that others that you thought were fine, have the same worries, is the best tonic.

At work, if you are not honest about how you feel, the unhappiness can eat away at you and eventually affect your home life and how you do your job. Any good manager should be there for their staff – happy people, who are happy in their jobs make the best employees – employers need to make more of an effort to know how their staff are feeling. It is no good waiting until you are about to lose a particularly good member of staff and then say, "Why didn't you tell me you were unhappy".

I bet many people reading this book, will have had that moment when you admit to a friend that you are worried about something, and it is making you unhappy, only to find that your confidant has the same worries. By the pair of you talking about the worry, you realise that you are normal, and that little speck of unhappiness is taken away, leaving you more room for happiness.

Being Happy Inside Out is not about avoiding the unhappy times – we all have them including me! The secret is that you need to acknowledge those unhappy times too and to recognise unhappiness.

Why am I talking about being unhappy in a book all about being happy some may ask, but that's real life! If people are honest with themselves, no one has a perfectly happy life all the time. The skill to being Happy Inside Out is being able to work through why you feel unhappy and doing something about that feeling of unhappiness, rather than accepting it. It is about how you respond to unhappiness. Allowing you to turn that unhappy feeling into a happy one. It does not always work but try it and you might surprise yourself.

When you have had a period of unhappiness, when you can turn it around or start feeling happy again, you appreciate the happiness more, and this sends a message to your brain that says, "I want more of this!" It is the Law of Polarity, for every down there is an up and this is how we learn and grow to understand our minds.

I know this book is about being Happy Inside Out but of course you are not going to be happy on the inside or the outside all the time. Being Happy Inside Out is not about avoiding the unhappy times. Unhappy times need to be acknowledged, as being Happy Inside Out is about responding to unhappiness in a way that allows you to grow from the experience and turn it into happiness.

Being happy is all about being able to forgive yourself, being able to laugh at yourself and the most important one, being able to understand yourself. Understanding what makes you happy and what does not, is key to being Happy Inside Out.

You will learn which people you feel happier around, where you like to go to feel happy, what you like to do. I am not saying avoid the people that make you feel unhappy but if you are aware of your thoughts and feelings then you can control the effect they have on you.

Being happy is not always easy. We must take responsibility for our own happiness and choose to concentrate on what we have and appreciate it, rather than what we do not have. No one else puts thoughts in your mind but you – it is your responsibility.

It is human nature to feel unhappy, but the important thing is to address why you are feeling that way.

- Is it a situation that has occurred?

- Could you have changed the outcome?

- Is it the people that you were with?

- Could you distance yourself from them in a subtle way to protect yourself from unhappiness?

Allow yourself to grow inside from the unhappiness and grow from the experience as you turn unhappiness into happiness. We are only human after all.

Being happy does not mean everything is perfect. It means you have decided to look beyond the imperfections. Focus on things you can control rather than worrying about things you cannot.

If you are feeling unhappy – you can be happy! Don't forget that.

A lovely lady called Lisa Hawkyard who is a Confidence Coach for women taught me this amazingly simple exercise which really works. Make a list of ten things that make you unhappy. Then write the opposite of each thing and think of a way to do, say, or change that unhappiness into happiness. I promise that just doing this simple exercise will make a difference to how you feel. Good luck x

Smiles

Turn that frown upside down – now that made you smile didn't it! If you look at a smiley face like the logo of this book and you really stare at it, you will eventually smile. The lovely thing about smiles is that they are free, and everyone can do it.

Sometimes we get so bogged down in our negative thoughts that we forget to smile. Don't forget to smile and aim to smile at something or someone at last once every day, even if that means smiling at yourself. It will make you feel so much better.

Ten things that might make you smile.

1. Looking at old family pictures

2. Finishing the last thing on your to do list

3. Seeing the faces of friends of family as they unwrap your presents for a Birthday or Christmas

4. Your favourite sports team winning an important match

5. Watching and seeing other people laughing and being happy

6. Having a hug

7. Kissing your children goodnight and being proud to be their parents

8. Thinking about something that made you smile in the past that you had forgotten about

9. Someone telling you a joke

10. Receiving a letter, message, or text from a good friend

Make sure you are the reason that someone smiles today. When you are going about your day, take the time to smile at people you meet. You do not know who may need a smile or what people are feeling. One thing for sure is that a smile from you, will make them feel happy inside, even if it's for a split second.

When you walk past people in the street, or even driving and stopping at traffic lights or a junction, smile at the people you have eye contact with and I guarantee that even if their day and thoughts are far from being happy, you will brighten their day for that brief moment. It will make you feel warm inside too when you hopefully receive a smile back.

Try it x

Happy Place

Where is your 'Happy Place'? Knowing your happy place is an important element of being Happy Inside Out.

I have talked a little about going to your happy place and doing this has helped me a lot over the years. My Happy Place when I was younger was playing my flute in the orchestra, being part of that whole team and creating whole experiences for the audience. I loved my music and could lose hours and hours playing my flute and piano. I was lucky, as it gave me the opportunity to visit foreign countries, which we had not done until I was 15 years old when I was growing up.

This brings me nicely to my other happy place, which is Pwll Du Headland and Brandy Cove Beach on the Gower in South Wales. For as long as I can remember, when I was young, we visited my grandparents as a family, and we would without fail always spend two weeks there in the Summer. Now as those of you may know that have visited South Wales, it sometimes rains a lot, and I can even recall spending hours and hours playing dominoes with my Grandad who had taught me. He used to cheat as there was a brown mark on the side of the six five domino, but we had lots of fun and dominoes always remind me of my Grandad Wright.

We would visit Brandy Cove and Pwll Du Headland most days, even if it were for a quick walk and we used to sing as we were walking and sometimes skip along the lanes that lead to both places. You cannot get to them by car, so you had to walk down the lanes and the two are joined by a cliff path, so if you were feeling very energetic, we used to do the whole circuit.

What was it that makes these my happy places – I think without a doubt the memories of those times. I love thinking about the sights we used to see along the way, the smells from the animals and sewage plant on route! And the many funny situations that happened along the way.

We used to go down to Brandy Cove beach and on sunny days stay down there all day, searching for star fish, building sandcastles and cars in the sand, swimming in the sea, playing cricket and popping into Mary's, which was my Nan's name and the name that she gave to a tiny hole in the towering rocks we visited if we needed a wee and couldn't face the sea. This opening was only accessible when the tide was out and is still there to this day. My Dad and Grandad would come down in the morning to help take everything down to the beach but then they would some days go back to the village (Bishopston) for a lunchtime beer in my Grandad's favourite pub The Valley, before heading back to the beach to help my Mum and Nan bring us and all our belongings home. Just writing this makes me smile x

When I lost my Grandad and then my Mum (quite suddenly), going to see my little Nan used to make me feel warm inside. We lost my Nan a few years ago and that connection to Brandy Cove and Pwll Du feels a little distant now. We will still go back, and it has been nice to take my children to the beaches and my niece and nephew and share some of our memories and make some of our own.

When I first lost my Mum, thinking of this happy place made me smile but with a tint of sadness, as it was somewhere I always went with my Mum and Dad. A few years passed and I have an updated 'happy place' which is our apartment in Spain. Why is it my happy place? We had thought about buying a home in Spain for many years, but we had never found the right place or had the capacity to do it.

When we viewed my happy place, it was wet and cold, the décor was frightful, and the owner had just cooked a paella but fast forward a year and it was now ours. I think what makes it my happy place is that I know how hard we have worked to have it – we can go there, and it is home from home. It is peaceful and friendly.

We have started to have lots of lovely, sometimes very funny memories of it with friends and family. When we arrive and wake up on that very first morning of sleeping there, I cannot wait to get up, put the coffee machine on and sit on the terrace looking at the view with the sun coming up and the birds singing. That is my happy place that I go to from the filing cabinet when I am feeling a little mewh. Have a coffee and imagine my happy place – it works every time.

My morning view from the kitchen of my happy place in Spain.

Having a happy place is particularly important if you want to be Happy Inside Out – what or where is your Happy Place? Think about it x

STOP

When you rush round and do not stop, you don't get a chance to recharge and when your batteries are low, that is when you become unhappy. It is OK to stop – whether it's for 5 minutes, 15 minutes or 55 minutes. Next time you are feeling stressed, stop and breathe in for three, hold for four and out for five. Try it, you are guaranteed to feel better.

When we are so busy, we can easily forget what makes us genuinely happy. It is not being lazy, just give yourself some time for 'you'. We all have different things that make us chill out and these are important. You would not expect a car to function at its best without a service, would you? Well, it is the same for you. Give yourself a break and you will feel so much better.

Think of how you feel if you are lucky enough to go on holiday. Yes, sometimes the getting there can add pressure to an already hectic life. But then when you are there and you relax, when you come home you are ready to get back to being busy because you have had a recharge.

If you are working so hard that you are always tired and grouchy, then think when you last gave yourself a day off. You do not have to do anything special on your day off – that is your choice, but the very action of spending some quality time with you, your friends or your family will make you feel so much better.

Work

Now most people must work, and it is a proven fact that we can spend more time at work than we do at home. When you look at the characteristics of successful people in business, there is one thing that is common with them all. They are happy working!

How many times have you heard friends, family or work acquaintances moaning about work? When you are in their company it is difficult to not allow their negativity to bring you down, but it is important that their negativity does not wear off on you. These negative moaners when asked if they are looking for a new job then, will say no and carry on moaning.

If you are unhappy at work, think about where you would like to work, is it a different profession? Look into it and see what's out there. Negativity at work will only wear you down and stop you from being genuinely Happy Inside Out.

In the past 20 years, the norm is no longer to stay in the same job or profession your whole working life. I once heard a headmistress explaining to a hall full of Year 7's (11-year-olds) that it is OK to change jobs and gave herself as an example – she used to sell mortgages but is now a very respected and successful head of a large academy trust.

If you are doing some team building or trying to teach younger children something, don't always focus on the negative things. For example, if you are in a work environment and are having a team meeting about customer service, ask the team to make a list of the positive feedback they receive from clients as well as the negative that may need working on. This will raise the mood, as all that are present will have that happy feeling of hearing the nice feedback and listening to the bad feedback that needs working on, will not be as tiresome.

To be truly Happy Inside Out, you need to be happy with your work. Perhaps not always doing the dream job you have always wanted to do but not a job that continually makes you sad and brings your energy and mood down x

Confidence

I could write a whole book on confidence and being self-confident but that is not the purpose of this book, but it is important to talk about it.

What do you think of when you see or hear the word confidence? To some it makes you think of the loudest person in the room or is it someone who always appears to be happy? Confident people inspire others but that does not mean they are self-confident.

If you think of your favourite sports person or film star, you may have heard them say that they have a special routine before a big match or making a speech. Everyone does something different, but they do this because it makes them feel happier inside and gives them the confidence to do the task in hand. To others it might sound strange, but it does not matter, do what feels right for you.

For me putting on my red lipstick gives me inner confidence and I like to think of this as my inner superpower. I'm not sure why but it gives me confidence inside to do whatever I am doing. Others might have lucky pants or must eat a particular food or do a certain exercise, but all these things are right and help your inner happiness protect you from not believing in yourself.

Always believe in yourself!

"I am enough"

Resilience

To achieve a feeling of happiness both inside and out, it is important to learn how to accept the current situation that you are in. What are you going to take forward as positives from the situation?

2020/21 is a great example of this with the Coronavirus COVID-19 pandemic. If you had told anyone at the start of 2020, that the whole world would be in lockdown and we would be forced to stay at home to work and play, have little face to face interaction with our nearest and dearest and it be illegal to travel outside of the UK, you would have thought that person was going mad!

Fast forward a year and that is exactly what has happened – quite unbelievable really. Many have used the time to do and learn new things which is how I came to be writing this book. It is very hard to believe that on 1 January 2020 I was lucky enough to be skiing in the beautiful resort of Whistler, Canada with my husband, son, and very good friends. Standing there in the queue for the ski lift with people from all over the world, all laughing and smiling – seems like an eternity ago but a lovely memory stored very safely in my memory folder of my filing cabinet.

I joined Michael Heppell's Write That Book Masterclass to gain new knowledge and top tips for how to market a book, being the Marketing and PR Consultant I am, and before I knew it, I was writing a book. Michael is one of the best speakers I have seen and is one of the world's leading personal development coaches. I thought about what I wanted to remember the 2020/21 lockdowns by and leave a legacy to my family and friends. "What did you do during the Coronavirus COVID-19 pandemic?" people will ask in the future and I will be proud to say, "I wrote a book!"

Why am I telling you this? Well, the reason is that I think of myself as quite a resilient person and although like many people, the Lockdowns of 2020 and 2021 had their highs and lows, they also taught me a lot about myself and my resilience.

I took the opportunity with both hands to do something that I love to do (write words) and use the current circumstances to create something that I hope will help others. If you accept the current situation that you are in and think how you can take the good and bad bits and use them to progress in the future, you are heading in the right direction that will lead to happiness – inside and out!

Your resilience helps you cope with the unhappy times and teaches you not only how to deal with them but also what to take from them to learn from. We are constantly learning from the time we are born to the moment we sadly pass away.

Give yourself time and focus on the good things that you can take forward. Some days it may be hard, but it is important.

Words

As I have said before I love words. Why do I love words – I am not sure. Lots of people underestimate the power of words. There is a quote by **Marcus Aurelius** which says:

"The happiness of your life depends upon the quality of your thoughts."

I and many others before me believe in taking this one step further and say that words lead to thoughts which become things. The words we use or do not use affect our happiness inside and out.

If someone constantly uses negative words to themselves or others, their mind becomes negative which leads to negative actions too. Now I am not saying we should all go around singing or chanting happy words all the time, as that would be rather silly (or mad!) and not build your resilience as we spoke about in the previous chapter.

When people use negative words all the time, the aura around them becomes negative and even toxic and this aura and presence can so easily brush off on others. Think back to when you have been in the company of someone that has just been negative the whole time moaning and using negative words. Then think back to when you have met someone, and that memory always makes you smile. Make sure you are always that second person that leaves a happy memory with people.

I saw this and it has stuck with me for years:

"Stressed"

Stressed is the word desserts spelt backwards! Now isn't that a nice thing to remember even if you are not a dessert person! So, the next time you feel stressed, think of your favourite dessert and I promise that will make you smile and feel a little happier inside.

If you are constantly told that you are no good at something, you start to believe that. Remember this if you are a parent or a manager of a team.

This is particularly important when talking to children and young adults. We should be helping them believe in themselves, their dreams and not always noticing things that they have done wrong. We must all learn, and this includes learning from the mistakes we make or the things we do wrong. When we become adults, we don't stop learning, we learn different things and it is from this learning that we all progress. If you speak to a successful person, they will say that they are always learning. We don't just learn at school or college, and we are not born with knowledge – we learn it.

Make a point of listening to the words you use regularly and if they are negative what would the positive be and focus on those. The first time I did this I was amazed – when I found myself thinking about saying something negative, I would stop and think of other ways to say it.

The words we use can pull us down without us even realising it. It is so important to think about the words you use not only when you speak but also when you write, whether that be for work in emails or letters, texts and even on social media.

If you genuinely want to be Happy Inside Out, then you must look at the words you use each and every day. Try it for a day and I bet you will be shocked at some of the words you use. Write them down and then at the end of the day read them and if they are negative words, write down the opposite and the next day try and use these new positive words and I promise they will make you feel warmer and happier inside.

You can use this in all areas of your life, whether it is talking to friends and family about your day, asking the children to do something, even speaking to your pets. Go on try it – words are extremely powerful.

To be Happy Inside Out, you need to be able to accept compliments and not to be too hurt by insults which are both words. Why is it that if someone pays us a compliment, we will probably forget it in a few days or weeks. However, if someone hurts you with an insult it can fester under the surface and in your mind for weeks, months or even years!

It is important to remember a compliment, or an insult is someone's opinion which they are entitled to have. Like happiness being unique so are opinions. Remember that the next time someone hurls an insult at you or pays you a compliment.

As many philosophers have said "It is not your business what others think of you."

Nurture

Nurturing our younger generation is especially important for all our futures. When you are young you may not get the results you wanted all the time or even at the end of your education, but this also builds your resilience, as we spoke about earlier. You can adapt your dreams and aspirations and who knows what the future holds.

"If I want to be free, I've got to be me, and living the life I want to be!"

As Oli Barrett MBE whose passion is connecting people and instilling belief into the younger generation said, "Most successful people don't go around being successful at everything, all day, every day."

This is so important to tell the younger generation who may be embarking on their next chapter after education. It is not all about exam results but about you as a person and what you feel, think and say. If you have a passion for something, have a go and don't be afraid if it doesn't go to plan, just as long as you learn from that experience and if the idea flies – well done you for having the courage to have a go.

Oli also says, "We all have a strength and something we can be brilliant at. The world is full of people that want to help you."

We have said this before, we are all unique – being brilliant can often be as unique to you as being happy. Don't follow the crowd, make your own brilliance. You will be so pleased that you did.

Don't be afraid to ask for help or guidance at any point in your life. When you reach out to people, yes, they may retract or ignore you, but they may also help you in a way that you could only have imagined or thought possible. I have always believed in the old saying:

If you don't ask, you don't get."

What is the worse someone can say? "No?"

Go on, give it a go.

Perception

"It's not who you are that holds you back, it's who you think you're not."

Denis Waitley

Now that is so true. The knowledge to do what you want to do is already here, it is the will that gives you energy to focus.

Sometimes we look at people and think how lucky they are to.... or how lucky they are having......, but remember happiness is different things to different people and we should never compare ourselves to others. This goes back to the point of us all being unique and different – concentrate on you and make yourself the best version of you.

Perception is how you see something and if you are striving to be or have something that is not you, you should ask yourself, will it really make me happy? When I first started work, I was lucky enough to get my first job at Coutts – the Queen's Bank. You have to have a lot of money to bank with them, but do you know what it taught me, and I was only in my late teens? Yes, sometimes money can help you along the way and make some opportunities more readily available to you, but rich people have the same problems but often they are just bigger versions of those problems.

You are the only one that can change you and you should live the way you want to live without the fear of being judged or ridiculed. If you dream of owning a big house in the country with lots of land and animals living off the fruits of our land that is fine. But equally, if you dream of having a little apartment in a cosmopolitan city living on your own and dining out most nights with friends and family, well that's OK too.

"It's not who you are that holds you back, it's who you
think you're not."

Denis Waitley

When you are feeling low and you do not know which way or who to turn to, go within. Sit quietly and go within to decide, use your initiative to see the answer and then act, so much better than a quick knee jerk reaction to something.

When something happens that may have shocked you, how you react or respond can have a big impact on not only to you but also to those around you. If you react to a situation, you lose control and a downward sad cycle can start, but if you respond and take one thing at a time and let the situation sink in, it gives your brain and inside time to respond and you will be in control.

"Respond don't react"

When a big drama happens, put it into perspective by concentrating on something of greater importance to you.

Know where you want to go in life, be that for relationships, friends, family, home, and work and the know will get you there. To get somewhere and make that change you must have the will to do it. Think of a runner – it is no good saying I want to run 5k but then telling yourself and everyone else that you hate running. You must have the will to run and then the running will get you to that 5K distance.

"You can't connect the dots looking forward, you can only connect them looking backwards. So, you have to trust that the dots will somehow connect in the future."

Steve Jobs

What a fantastic quote from Steve Jobs. You must remember that there is no limit to where you can go x

"You can't connect the dots looking forward, you can only connect them looking backwards. So, you have to trust that the dots will somehow connect in the future."

Steve Jobs

Rebalance

If you are feeling a little sad, just remember that you are human and that this blip of unhappiness is your energy inside being out of alignment.

Think of this feeling as being like when you are walking along a tree trunk in the woods on a nice walk – if you wobble, it does not mean you are going to fall off (cannot be happy), it just means you need to concentrate a bit more on being happy and rebalance.

If you just give up, you will fall off and be unhappy for longer, but I genuinely believe a little blip or slip every now or then is natural and sometimes needed to rebalance, as it is part of your growth towards being genuinely happy both inside and out x

Look at what has made you sad, understand and learn from it.

"Turn that frown upside down!

Be strong, but not rude

Be kind, but not weak

Be bold, but not a bully

Be humble, but not shy

Be proud, but not arrogant"

Jim Rohn

When you write something down, you are setting the intention to do it, make it happen.

When you start to let go of things that do not serve you, you are making space for something bigger and better.

Just do it! There is no time like the present and waiting just makes you feel older and more anxious. Look after you and then you can look after others.

"Be strong, but not rude

Be kind, but not weak

Be bold, but not a bully

Be humble, but not shy

Be proud, but not arrogant"

Jim Rohn

Moving Forward

When we think about being happier, we often say to ourselves that we need to make changes. Sometimes we put too much pressure on ourselves thinking that we must make huge changes, and this is where it goes wrong.

We have very good intentions to make changes that we think will make us happier inside and out but often we fall at the first hurdle. Those changes sound good, but they very quickly feel like they are a step too far and we give up or admit defeat.

I think that to make changes for yourself, you have to work on yourself to really make a difference. Don't make the easy mistake of thinking about all the things that would make you feel happier inside and out as big challenges and changes. It is far better and you will see greater and longer lasting results, if you see these changes you would like to make as little steps moving forward. Your mind associates moving forward with progress.

Think back to when you were a toddler or your children being toddlers. When they learn to walk you do not expect them to run a marathon in the first weeks they start to walk. In fact, you do not even expect them to run, it is all about taking little steps to move you forward in the right direction.

When you think of little changes that you could make in your life, home, work, attitude, words, thoughts, friends, family – in fact, all the things that we have been talking about, little changes move you forward. That is the most important thing to remember! Little steps moving forward to your goal will make an impact and often a bigger impact than you think they will.

These little steps do not need to be massive things. It could be as simple as making a conscious effort to smile at one person today or making that one phone call to a friend or relative that you have not spoken to for ages or even giving yourself 5 minutes of 'me' time one day a week to start with.

All these little steps will lead you to bigger achievements and your goal of being happier inside out. Everyone is different, so don't worry about how big your changes are that you feel you need to do. Remember we are all unique and the little steps and changes that one person can do on their journey to happiness inside and out, will be vastly different to someone else.

These minor changes you make are all a step in the right direction, and that is good. If I said to you, "right we need to organise the whole house this weekend," you would probably eye roll and think "well that's not going to happen." But if I said "We are going to organise a room a weekend from now on" you would be much more likely to have a go, as it does not sound like such a huge challenge.

I use this example as I did this in the first COVID-19 national lockdown. I needed to organise bedrooms as we were moving my son into what was the playroom/office which sounds quite easy. But to do that I needed to sort the playroom/office for him to move to, then move the spare bedroom to his old bedroom and then move my office to the old spare room! It filled me with dread, as it is amazing what a family of four can accumulate in the 9 years we have lived in our present house.

I had been putting it off, as it just seemed such a huge job but when I thought about it as stages of what I could do and accepted that I could not do it all in one weekend, it became more manageable, and it got done!

Another example of this is when it comes to exercise. At the beginning of 2020, I decided to do the Couch to 5K Challenge on a Running Machine. Now I have never run before and wanted to give it a go.

The thought of running 5K was extremely daunting and filled me with dread, but the way that the app I was using built up the time you ran for, started to make it more manageable. I am immensely proud that I persevered and managed to complete the challenge. When it came to the final runs of the challenge, I still had to break it up into smaller achievements of 10 minutes in my head or my legs would have stopped but breaking it up, made it easier to achieve in my head and it worked.

Do whatever works for you. Take some time to write down some of the things that you want to get done. Now look at the biggest goal and write down three or more goals that when put together will see you achieving the big goal. Now it may be that there has to be one medium goal and several little ones, but I promise you that this makes larger goals easier to achieve. The sense of achievement and inner happiness it brings as you not only cross off those 'To Do's' but also know that you are moving forward towards that bigger goal, is what makes you feel happier inside out.

Make sure you find time for you each and every day, even if it is just for 5 minutes. Try and use that time to calm your mind and relax. In this crazy world and 2020/2021 so far, has certainly been crazier than previous years, we are all so busy rushing around here and there, thinking of the next place we need to be at or the next job we need to do.

Just STOP – open that filing cabinet in your mind and bring out your happy place and breathe. Just shut your eyes and imagine yourself in your happy place – what does it look like? What does it feel like? How does it make you feel? I bet it makes you smile! I promise that at the end of the 5 minutes, you will feel happier inside, calmer, and ready for whatever you need to do or wherever you need to go next.

Happiness is about being you! There is only one of you, so enjoy it and be Happy Inside Out!

Part 2

INCEspiration

This section of the book is about my method of helping you be Happy Inside Out with some of the things I think you need to think about, and it is called INCEspiration:

Imagination

Nurture

Choice

Expectation

Success

Positivity

Intuition

Repetition

Attitude

Trust

Inspire

Originality

Now

Use my INCEspiration method like you would a recipe to make a cake – use all the ingredients to help you be Happy Inside Out. Good luck x

I is for Imagination

Often when people hear the word imagination, they think back to their childhood when they used their imaginations to write stories or play games with their friends. They say that children are like sponges as not only do they absorb information, but they also crave it too.

I think that if we really think about it, we don't stop being sponges when we grow up – instead, we have a longing to stretch our imagination but because we have grown up and life comes along, sometimes this stops us from growing our minds and using our imagination because of work, family etc.

If you think about it, as we grow up, all that really happens is that we use our imagination for different things such as our dream job, our ideal partner, our perfect house – the list is endless.

What we need to do is use our imagination to grow and fulfil our dreams. We may not be able to make all our dreams come true, but we can use our imagination to adapt them and without a doubt this will lead to you feeling happy inside and out.

N is for Nurture

Many great philosophers believe that our past affects our future. That our childhood, the people around us and the words that are used when we are young greatly affect the person that you are today.

I do believe this to be true to a certain extent, but I also honestly believe that you can make your own happiness. Just because you have always done or said something a certain way, it doesn't mean that you cannot change that.

I am passionate about nurturing the young people of today and letting them create their own characters and voice. There is a lot of pressure on children to get great results at the present time, but how often is the pressure from schools and colleges for the benefit of the children? There is an exceptionally fine line between pressure for good results being about our future generations or is it about the school results and their reputation?

There has been lots of press around mental health in the last few years and even more in this crazy year we call 2020. Children have had no school or college for months on end and the pressure to do well, to get the right grades, is I think, more than ever.

What about the self-belief of that same young generation? If all they hear is pressure from school and college, their parents and family and the media about exam results and having to succeed with the highest grades to be successful, then that is going to affect how they feel and think of themselves.

They may have a dream of doing something completely different or perhaps, which I think is much more common, are not sure what they would like to do in the future, then we should be helping them, not destroying their imaginations and dreams.

Yes, it is important to try your best and that is what we should be saying to our young people. If they want to be the next greatest footballer or be an astronaut – don't let anyone say they can't. It is important to dream.

Again, it comes back to words. If you are constantly told that you are no good at something or you must try harder, then you will struggle to turn those words into positive actions. How many young people do you know that may not have been the most successful pupils at school but are now well and truly on their way to being extremely successful.

When Formula 1 Champion Lewis Hamiton won his 7th World Championship in 2020, he stood there as he was interviewed just after the race and said,

"Follow your dreams, speak them into existence"

Now that for me was motivational, no matter what your age or the stage of your life you are at.

There are many, in fact too many to mention, extremely successful people who come from very humble beginnings, whether that be in the world of sport or business. When you study them, what is it that they all have in common? They had a dream and they worked extremely hard to fulfil that dream.

When you follow your dreams, it is so important to remember that it is not always going to be about success and happiness. Some of the happiest people inside and out would probably not call themselves successful at all, but they are happy. As we said at the beginning of the book, happiness means different things to different people and that is what you need to remember.

C is for Choice

We all have a choice, and we make hundreds of choices every day, often without even realising it. You choose which foot to get out of bed first thing every morning – now I bet you would not have said that was one of your first choices of the day.

We can choose to accept things, or we can change them – that is your choice. People often say they don't have a choice, but you do. Do you choose to be happy? Everyone would surely choose that, but perhaps you choose to be sad and that is sometimes the right choice too, as by feeling sad you are thinking about what is making you sad, rather than trying to ignore it and not understanding it. If you try to understand why something might make you sad for example, that will lead to a new choice, which could lead to happiness, but will also make you wiser to the thing that made you sad.

If you are unsure of which direction to go, listen to your heart, your heart will help you make the right choice. Sometimes people spend ages making a choice and then miss out on something or make several choices but then come back to the first choice they made. There is no right or wrong – just be true to yourself with the choices that you make.

Some people wonder why the same things happen to them repeatedly and things don't change even if they want them to. The problem here is that they are doing the same thing repeatedly which always leads to the same results.

The key is choice – you have the choice to change so that you can achieve a different result but too often it is so much easier to just carry on doing the same thing and hope for a change – NO! Make the choice to get different results and change what you need to. These changes may be big or small and both are fine, but it is important to make sure you make the right choice to change.

Think of a marathon runner trying to improve his performance time. If he or she runs the same way, chances are their performance time will remain the same or at best improve a little. However, if they make the choice to change the pace, how they start or how they finish, then the result, i.e., their performance, will change and they will get the result they are looking for.

This choice can work for anything – relationships, work, health, weight, and happiness. Don't decide to change and then carry on the same way, or all you will do is make yourself unhappy again, as chances are you will be seeing the same results. Make that choice to stick to those changes and see the results you are looking for. When you see the results, that will make you happier.

E is for Expectation

You expect to be happy, but you don't know what to do? If you don't know what makes you happy, then how are you going to turn those unhappy thoughts into happy ones.

Philosophers have always said that if you are unhappy but expect to be happy doing and thinking the same way you always have, then you cannot expect to see or feel any changes or be happy. You need to move forward in all you do. Don't dwell on the past but make sure that you always learn from experience.

The Cambridge English Dictionary has this definition of the word Expectation,

"The feeling or belief that something will or should happen"

Another way of looking at it, is that you need to ask yourself what you are expecting from work, family, friends, or yourself. It is no good expecting something and then being disappointed when it doesn't happen if you haven't done anything to help make it happen. Sometimes things need working at, or slight changes need to happen to fix things, or perhaps what is needed is a little give and take of the situation to turn it in the right direction. Sometimes we can just simply expect too much but it is so important to recognise this.

"Act without expectation."
Lao Tzu

"Act without expectation."
Lao Tzu

S is for Success

Some people feel that success must be a huge achievement or step, but in truth it doesn't have to be. The person that has just won a £1million contract for his business is just as successful as the person that has depression and has managed to get out of bed in the morning. This is so important to remember.

It stems from our childhood and being at school, we are told repeatedly that success is doing well in our exams, but I think we can be as successful being ourselves as individuals, just as much as we can be successful at exams. We are all different.

What does success mean to you? Think about this when you look at what makes you happy. Amongst some of the most successful people in your eyes, I can guarantee that not all of them may be happy. Once again it comes back to the fact that we are all unique and have different values and beliefs.

I believe that being Happy Inside Out makes you successful. It means that you know what makes you happy, you know what makes you sad, and you know how to deal with that unhappiness and try and turn it around to happiness.

If one person reading this book feels they are truly happier inside and out, then I will know that this book has been a success. For me, it is not about writing a No.1 Best Seller, the number of books I sell, or if I make any money from it – it is about helping others and the best feeling that comes when you know you have done that. That will make me Happy Inside Out! It's about looking after yourself, believing in yourself, and your happiness is the success.

P is for Positivity

I could write a whole book on positivity! Are you a glass half full or half empty sort of person?

We have all been around those people that say, "You will never be able to do that" or "I know that's not going to work." or "You will never get to be an astronaut." Again, it is about words, be positive! Surely, it is better to say that you have had a go at something or tried to make something work rather than thinking "what if…?"

If you go around saying you are unhappy, then your whole aura is going to be negative, you will start using negative words and then your energy will dip……I could go on. Being positive is a much better way of looking at life.

If you do not give something a go, then how will you know if it doesn't work, or you can do something or be the person you want to be. Much better to be able to say that you had a go, you gave it a good dash of positivity and if it wasn't meant to be, perhaps that is the right outcome, but you will undoubtably feel much better that you had a go.

"If it's to be, it's up to me."

William H Johnsen

Positive people have positive minds, take positive actions, use positive words, and mix with other positive people. It is a little like following a recipe to make a cake!

If you want to be positive but you use lots of negative words, it is almost impossible to be completely positive, no matter how much positive action, or positive people you are mixing with. The recipe of being a success and being positive will only be truly achieved if all the ingredients are used. If you think you are a positive person already, then by making a slight change to acknowledge the words that you find yourself using, will make you realise that you can be even more positive.

"If it's to be, it's up to me."

William H Johnsen

I is for Intuition

Intuition is a funny thing - I think that it plays a part in your happiness. Intuition is the feeling you get in your belly/bones that something is right or wrong. Some would say you know the truth or what to do by the way it feels. How many times have you heard someone say, "I had a feeling that would happen, I could feel it in my bones,"

The definition of intuition is an immediate understanding or knowing something without reasoning - You know or understand something without reasoning or proof. Sometimes, your heart may be telling you to do something, but your inner soul is saying something else. Your heart can be swayed too which is where the saying "Love is blind" comes from.

To be happy with something that you want to do, or are about to do, you should trust your intuition as it is usually right. Sometimes our brains can be brainwashed with other factors, such as something that people have said, you can see things that may sway your decision or have read things related to your decision but if you stop and think, you will know what the right decision is and which way you should go. Do not be easily influenced by your surroundings, go with your gut, and do what you think is the right choice for you.

To be genuinely Happy Inside Out, you must trust your intuition as it is linked. Sometimes it is easier to do something to make a problem go away or say yes to something, even if it doesn't sit right with your feelings inside. Have the strength and confidence to trust your inner soul and do what it is telling you.

R is for Repetition

As you make the conscious effort to do all the things, we have spoken about in your endeavour to be Happy Inside Out, you are creating new habits. Your motivation to be Happy Inside Out is a feeling and therefore temporary as it can disappear. When your motivation to be happy disappears, you are left with routine, discipline, and habits.

If you make sure that your habits, when you are motivated to be happy, are strong, and part of your routine of life in your mind and your body, then through repetition, they will still be there when you are not motivated and perhaps unhappy. Habits help to produce your outcomes and progress makes us happy. We all know that you must get the basics right to enjoy the exciting bits don't we.

Repetition is key and any coach whether that is a personal coach, a fitness coach, a mindset coach or even a business coach will tell you that you can only change when you repeat the exercises, procedures, mindset that you learn.

Some say that it takes 30 days for something to feel more natural and not a chore and some say it takes 90 days. A little like happiness, we are all unique and it can take every one of us a different time.

By thinking about what makes you happy or not and doing the little things we have talked about in this book, you have a greater understanding of yourself and that is what this is all about. You learn what makes you happy or unhappy so that when you are unhappy you know what to do to try and be happy again.

A is for Attitude

What is Attitude? Your attitude is made up of your thoughts, feelings, and actions. Happiness is a thought, so if you are feeling unhappy you can change that thought into a happy one by thinking of something that makes you feel happy. The action you take is turning that unhappy thought into a happy one.

I am sure you have heard of the phrase of someone having a "can do" attitude. What this means is that when someone is asked to do something, they automatically think they can do it as a positive, rather than almost give up before they have started.

Being Happy Inside Out requires you to have a positive attitude but that doesn't just mean you are always right. It means that your happiness and positiveness come through in your thoughts, your feelings, and your actions and that is when you see results. It is not saying that you must be smiley and happy all the time, more that you are in control of your emotions and know exactly what makes you happy and how to learn to turn around or more importantly learn from any unhappiness that comes your way.

T is for Trust

When we speak about trust, it is not only about trusting other people but also about trusting yourself. It goes back to intuition and that you should trust how you feel, what you say and what you do.

Trust and believe in yourself and other people. We are unique yes, but because we are all unique it means that sometimes we need to trust other people to help us be happy. After all you cannot be happily married on your own can you!

Trust in your feelings of doing the right thing, having the right thoughts, and following the right paths. Trust is so important as it holds things together.

I is for Inspire

Inspire yourself as well as others. Often when people think about inspiration, they think it only applies to how we make other people feel, but it is so important to inspire ourselves too. We are important and it is a crucial part of being Happy Inside Out that we inspire ourselves as well as others.

Has someone said to you "You really inspire me"? If you are lucky enough to have that said to you, then without a doubt hearing those words would give you that tingly feeling of happiness inside and out. Do not ever be embarrassed if someone says that to you, as it is a real compliment. I think to be considered an inspiration is an honour and a great achievement – something to be proud of.

We inspire to be like someone because we admire them. They make us feel good, they make us feel happy and this is a good thing. It might be the job that they do, the resilience they show in troubled times, it can be a whole host of things.

O is for Originality

We have said it before but there is only one of you. If we were all the same life would be very boring and we would not learn from each other.

It is important to be happy with you – what does that mean I hear you say. If we are not genuinely happy with the kind of person we are, then we will never truly be content. You don't have to be like this person or that person, just be you.

Write down the qualities that you feel you have, and I bet you will be surprised at some you write down. If you then asked friends and/or family what they thought your qualities were, they may produce the same list or they may produce something different, that you have not recognised in yourself. Focusing on your qualities and strengths is so much better than just focussing on your weaknesses.

There is only one of you so learn to embrace you. Give yourself a pat on the back when you have a good day, you are allowed to. Sometimes we are so busy and intent on being like somebody else, that we forget who we are and that's when unhappiness can creep in and stop you from feeling Happy Inside Out.

Be the person you truly are, and you will not only be happier inside and out, but you will also radiate more happiness wherever you go and whoever you are with.

Now is for Now

If you do the same thing and have the same unhappy thoughts and feelings week after week you will get the same unhappy thoughts. Do it now, not tomorrow, not in a minute, not next......... (how many times have I caught myself saying these!)

Without taking action, you will not get results. So, if you genuinely want to feel happier inside and out, make the changes now. You do not want to be the person that tip toes through life wanting to make it safely to death and always saying "well it's OK, I will be happy when......"

It is much better to live your life now, being the person, you want to be. Remember the changes that you need to make do not have to be enormous life changing events but so much better to take little steps forward in the right direction. Lots of little steps will lead to some big achievements and moments of happiness inside and out.

DO IT NOW! xx

Part 3

Happy and Inspirational Quotes

I have always loved quotes and find them extremely inspirational. It amazes me how you think you have a favourite quote and then one day you find another. I think it is important to have a library of quotes to be able to call upon in any situation.

As we are all unique, quotes often mean different things to different people too but I thought it important to have a section of my book about being Happy Inside Out with some of my personal favourite quotes. I hope they speak to you too.

Visit my website: www.happyinsideout.co.uk for more inspirational quotes.

"Some days I feel happy,
Some days I feel sad,
And some days I'm not sure how I feel,
And that can make me feel quite mad.

But then I make sure I speak to 'me'
All you can do is your best,
If your best isn't good enough for something,
Let it be and get on with the rest!"

Andrea Ince

"If it's to be, it's up to me."

William H Johnsen

"If we do what we are able to do today, it will open the way for us to do something better tomorrow."

'Yourself' from The Hidden Power by Thomas Troward

"If you don't go after what you want, you'll never have it. If you don't ask, the answer is always no. If you don't step forward, you're always in the same place."

Nora Roberts, Author

"I am enough"

"Be yourself; everyone else is already taken."

Unknown

"Follow your dreams, speak them into existence."

Lewis Hamilton

"Yesterday is history, tomorrow is a mystery, but today is a gift. That's why they call it the present."

Unknown

"Happy people are beautiful.
They become like a mirror and they reflect happiness."

Drew Barrymore

"Make sure you are the reason someone smiles today."

"If I want to be free, I've got to be me, and living the life I want to be!"

"It's not who you are that holds you back, it's who you think you're not."

Denis Waitley

"Imagination is more important than knowledge."

Einstein

"Focus on things you can control rather than worrying about things you cannot change."

"If you have good thoughts, they will shine out of your face like sunbeams, and you will always look lovely."

Roald Dahl

"Stop waiting for Friday,
For Summer,
For someone to fall in love with you,
For Life,
Happiness is achieved when you stop waiting for it and
make the most of the moment you are in now."

"Happiness is not by chance but by choice."

Jim Rohn

"Create your own sunshine."

"Make happiness a habit."

"Don't let silly little things steal your happiness."

"Happiness is not something ready-made. It comes from your own actions."

Dalai Lama

"Being happy never goes out of style."

Lilly Pulitzer

"When nothing goes right, go left."

"Happiness depends upon ourselves."

Aristotle

"Be happy, and a reason will come along."

"Being happy doesn't mean everything's perfect. It means you've decided to look beyond the imperfections."

"The key to being happy is knowing you have the power
to choose what to accept and what to let go."

Dodinsky

"If you want to be happy, be."

Leo Tolstoy

"Life is short, always choose happiness."

"The most important thing is to enjoy your life - to be happy – it's all that matters."

Audrey Hepburn

"Tomorrow will be a good day."

Captain Sir Tom Moore

"Kindness in words creates confidence
Kindness in thinking creates profoundness
Kindness in giving creates love."

Lao Tzu

"Sometimes the smallest things take up the most room in your heart."

Winnie the Pooh

"Keep your face to the sunshine and you cannot see the shadows. It's what sunflowers do."

Helen Keller

"Happiness is letting go of what you think your life is
supposed to look like."

"It is not how much we have, but how much we enjoy,
that makes happiness."

Charles Spurgeon

"Be your own kind of beautiful."

"It is far more exciting
To create a miracle
Than to wait for one
To happen."

"Be brave and follow what YOU believe instead".

"The happiness of your life depends upon the quality of your thoughts."

Marcus Aurelius

"The only thing that will make you happy, is being happy with who you are, and not who people think you are."

Goldie Hawn

"Nothing is impossible. The word itself says, "I'm possible."

Audrey Hepburn

"There are only two days in the year that nothing can be done.
One is called yesterday,
The other is called tomorrow.
Today is the right day to love, believe,
Do, and mostly Live."

"Be yourself; everyone else is already taken!"

Oscar Wilde

"When you get attached to the result
You miss out on all the magic."

"Don't worry
About a thing
For every little thing
Gonna be all right."

Bob Marley

"Don't let yesterday take up too much of today."

"Happiness is not about something ready-made,
It comes from your own actions."

"When you buy from a small business, an actual person does a happy dance."

"I am what I ask for
I am what I believe
What comes after I am is the strongest I will ever be."

"When life gets you down,
You know what you gotta do?
Just keep swimming......!"

Dory the Fish

"Happiness is letting go of what you think your life is supposed to look like and enjoying it for everything that it is."

Mandy Hale

"Don't let the noise of others' opinions drown out your inner voice.
And most important have the courage to follow your heart and intuition.
They already know what you truly want to become".

Steve Jobs

"Don't stress,
Do your best!"

"Life is like a balloon!
If you never let yourself go,
You will never know how far you can rise!"

"Always remember
You are braver than you believe,
Stronger than you seem,
And smarter than you think."

Christopher Robin

"Do what makes you happy!"

"Learn to enjoy every minute of your life. Be happy now!"

Earl Nightingale

"Act without expectation."

Lao Tzu

"The secret of happiness is low expectation."

Barry Schwartz

"Whether you think you will succeed or not, you are right."

Henry Ford

"Most people are about as happy as they make up their mind to be."

Abraham Lincoln

"You can't connect the dots looking forward, you can only connect them looking backwards. So, you have to trust that the dots will somehow connect in the future."

Steve Jobs

About the Author

Andrea Ince is 50 years old and lives and works in Essex, UK. She is a married mum of two young adults and a successful PR and Marketing Consultant. Andrea has always been a great advocate of personal development and has almost 30 years of marketing and PR experience in many sectors and loves helping other people.

"Seeing people grow and succeed that you have helped is a great feeling. I am always promoting something for somebody else but wanted to do something for me."

"I am a strong believer in being yourself and not what you think you should be like or what others may think you should be. Through my own personal development journey, I finally feel that I am Happy Inside Out and if this book helps one person learn to have that same feeling, then that makes me Happy Inside Out too!"

"The book also leaves a legacy for my family and friends that can be adapted for the future. What did you do in the lockdowns of 2020/21 people will ask in the future, and I will be proud to say I wrote a book!"